And he says I have this hardly-original
hole inside of me; that I am two things
infinitely: carnal and futile. He's right.
I am a bad wife, a wanting quarry
of witless worry; lank rage, grim schlock,
and stroppy poverty. I am sleazed in
the green of The Land, raining down
her birdsong in blows. The dubby
crush of my keening does his head in.
I sink kisses into screams like pushing
pennies into mud. And he says he is *done*.
From the wordy murk of my loss come
lanterns and daggers, and I am my country:
mean, gutless and Medieval; a dread
mess of battlements and spoils. He cannot
love me, grieved to my gills and grinding
exile like an axe. He cannot love me,
howling out my mutant blues to no one.
My semi-automatic sobbing wakes
the neighbours. I am sorry. I have tried
to live lightly, to live like *gadje* girls,
to make my mouth an obedient crock
of homage; to keep my swift hands soft
in illiterate peachiness. But I am from
an ugly world, an ugly world with ugly
songs for busking in an underpass. I am
not one your machine-washable muses,
my face a cotton swab. I cannot come
clean, come cosy, come tame and fond.
His suckling fund of human love destroys
me. I am not good. I am a ferreting girl
who steals from shops, a perfidious febrile
girl who gobs off bridges; a hedging
and fretting girl, one eye on the exit.

I am *terrible.* I drink myself to a fly-
tipped farrago of falling down. No decorum
in me. My mourning is eloquent strumpetry,
and ruin porn will always be the whole
of my Law. I am sorry. And he says he
cannot love me in my insolent libidiny;
my shrill pandemic ditties: poems bleating
like woebegone ringtones. He cannot love me
in my words, raptures dragged from the slangy
wastes of Norn. He says he will have none,
when a poem is a viral fire that spreads my anger
round; a typo-tastic war grave in which I bury
my dead. And he says I am *damaged.* I frisk
the heart for sadness, find it waiting
like a toothache. It is true. Thrice fool girl,
dangled at a day's end, what have I got
besides? There is only this particular fire
in me, this brief biotic craze of light, a halo
like a yellow enzyme: luciferase, fanatical,
and *dragging us down*, he says. He leaves
and slams the door. I breathe again. The T.V
leaks a sour myrrh meaning evening. I scuff
my breath on the edges of an empty room.
Here is the moon, poor feme sole,
and the orange stars in their cold swoon.

Euterpe, 1953

I should tread carefully; these village women envy
me my revels, and when the Ten Bells has called time
their husbands come, to sway like charmed snakes
on the green. They come to drink poitín, to weave
and rail among the harebells and the broom. They come
to me, and I will not refuse them. I am all they have
of music.

And all men must have music, those young bucks bailing a song
from the depths of their bellies like water from a sinking boat;
even their fathers, starched in isinglass and prayer, who live
by discipline and thrift, for omens and for rosaries. They have
need of music too, for the swift physic of a poem; for shanties,
canting, bawdy psalms, all liming the throat like scalded milk.

I step into the centre of a circle in my silks, my skirts skirl
and madden, and the darkness dares a dance; the sky is crazy-
paved with stars. My hands are a hotbed of sovvies. I gather
my garlands and thalers, and twist, red and orange, inflammable
abandon. My flute blooms like a thorn-apple, pollenates an air
from woozy succour and rare night breath.

And we begin to surge and solve in rhythm. My music is
the flesh laid bare; the body is a song made flesh. The men
are getting creaturely, their voices peeled and keening out
in tune. This ransacked swim of heat and sweat is all we have
to prove we live. And I will corrugate praise in the teeth of dying.
Lament is a false friend. Revel is an engine, pumps the blood.

But I should tread carefully; these village women envy
me my revels, and when their husbands skulk to cold beds,
old scores and cold mutton, I'm alone, and I know well
how each kiss to its repercussion travels. In the early light
of morning those pious biddies throw their stones, the menfolk
holding torches as my gleaning dance unravels. Ever thus, but
when they come, then I will not refuse them. No, I will not
refuse them, I am all they have of music.

Thalia

I couldn't decide whether to get a tattoo of a pegasus or a unicorn
and he says it's not *a* pegasus it's just Pegasus capital P definite article
and so I say well what is the name for a winged horse then?
and he didn't know and anyway in the end I went and plumped for
a wicked corolla of violet stars.

This other time his mouth a boozy gizmo pressing into mine and the boys
at the bus stop Jason especially langered long tongues out a country mile
and perving away without whit one of shame and so busy looking up my
skirt they didn't see Mad Ganley coming along the road his scrumpy face
skinned by the moonlight as it were an apple peeled to reveal its brown bits
and nasty bruises.

And I think it's better to be merry don't you? and I was snaking and laddering
and he was coming alive like a rope trick under my hands and I said I don't
love you love you or anything but please baby be my fifth business and he was
pressing on my freckles like he was keying in his pin and my body was this big
fleshy ATM or something and I opened my mouth and laughed and I half
expected a pageant of sodden fivers to fly out and hit him in the face.

Best of all though best of all though best of all is the girls my sisters
when we go out all shiny eyes and Dimonique drinking our trinkety skinful
and our forte is floozy and rare auld times and in the fluorescing plenty
of the club when we're writhing as one like a Hindu deity so many pairs
of bangled wrists hennaed hands and *he* says kiddo I wish there was more
of me to go round and I sing never ever such devoted sisters and we're
gorged on the dance spliffy vixens going down in an April shower of hijinx
giggles and cheap Lambrini.

Clio

My mother was a Goddess, ash blonde
and sombre longing; she kept a *wise tongue.*

When memory was sewage
treatment work, the water lapped
over her elbows like opera gloves;
she wore green velvet and white
feathers- lushly augmented.

Her perfume was mock orange, zinnia,
syringa. Her nails were perfect; her breath
a wrangle of flowers.

My mother held on to our history - pinkly
strombus conch clutching the sound of the sea.

My mother was a Goddess, and when
she spoke a yellow light embellished
her head in a soft cartoon *Eureka!*

My mother whispered *home* and *road*
with the same exhausted tenderness
as old men blowing their warm
air into the nose of a spooked horse.

I am not my mother.
I must bawl and crow,
pulling the past from my head
like a hank of hair.

My wet brain is whoopee-squeezed
or wrung out as a damp rag.
I fathom like a fishwife, live by *ruckus*
and by *flannel*; spring our stories
on strangers, clucking my shameless
payload patois-loony on the bus.

Poshrat, history is the sucked egg
my mouth won't hold. I have to speak
or else snap mad.

Oh, here are our ancestors, wide in all
their inundating deadness. They shriek
through me, or else I teem, ghostbusy.

I must speak of this, our dead,
swaying in an amnesty of bandages
and indefensible deeds.

They come by cudgel and succour,
by gutrot, gouging and secret melee.

The dead will sing, a slurred flurry
of voices, slurry of voices. They are
a chorus for gallows and lynchings.

A hanged man is a string instrument.
An ogre beating his wife like a drum.

My mother was a Goddess, she could charm
bees and her cheekbones were stunning.
Her silence gathered dust like an heirloom.

I am an unquiet child. I see things
and I must tell:

That man, grinning out from under
the redacted oblong of his eyes, crawled
from the comic opera of the past, dragging
his period costume;

the shimmering child, a mirage,
his upturned face is filling with sleep.
A plastic basin fills with rain.

Erato

I'm Miss World, somebody kill me
– Hole, *Miss World.*

And to top it all off, I'm expected to ride on
a float, my face scraped on in a strong wind, all
tits and teeth, rigid as any a hood ornament: winged
Victory, pigtailed and pinioned. Bow to the crowd
like Jackie O, glamming it up at an airport. Blow
them a kiss, sceptred Gretchen, bestowing my lip-
gloss right and left. Pah! Nothing's changed.
I could be one of those big-boned comely undulants
from back in Nana's day, a greyscale girl in stiff sateen,
rubbing the suds from her smile. Same naff spangles
anyway, same paste tiara, dollop face, congenial
and mooning. But oh, those were *healthy* girls, curly
and fey and easily pleased. Nana, with her Fanta-
shock of orange hair, pale as a plate of pressed curd;
a rosette pinned to her rubbery dugs by the mayor.
Yuck! The windy bag of his jowls an inch from her
upturned nose, and he gropes like a mole at her seed-
pearled bodice. Nana, a gattling girl, content to prate
world peace and happy marriage till the cows came
lowing home. But I am not *healthy*, not *happy*, not safe
in the jammy past. I am myself, and only myself:
specimen of soothsaid youth, the dispensable
and disarranged. My bones lack calcium. My life
lacks direction. I am only myself, prized from the ant-
farm farce of social housing, and held to the light
like a counterfeit coin. A brazen fake and everybody
knows it. Not *lovely* but *typical*. A karaoke beauty,
only fit for generic reels and green streamers.
My compact mirror shows a sad wan, cornered
by exhaustion, too tired to turn being stared at
into an art form. Gawp at the camera. Pink pout
pops in a flashbulb like gum.

Urania/Ourania

Tonight there is a storm and Reverend Mother
has confiscated all our magazines!

Reverend Mother, in the half-light through her open
door, looks like a thin, green candle. She carries
a patterned birch and a psalter, God and his much-
gilded invective.

Because she took our magazines I will do the casting. I am
better than the magazines, their guesswork and dappy fashions.
When you turn over the cards you must keep your Fate Hand
steady. It is like playing Operation. No, it is like taking an eyelash
out of your own eye with needle-nosed tweezers.

Tonight there is a tempest, as in *The Tempest*, and I
am casting. First I must shut up my swarmy thoughts.
I disappear into the vanity cabinet – skin diver pursuing
a pearl, a pill, a plaintive string of pills, lined up in
a long chain, hoaxing a rosary.

Now I am ready. Tonight the island is wild.
A cormorant is a silk purse for a portion of storm.
I watch the cormorants fold away their wings, closing
up their bodies like gibbets. Such auguries! My head is
hollow with vision. My thoughts caught in the halogen
strip like flies. I am wearing my own hair as a hood.
I am going to begin my predictions:

Tonight there will be hurricanes! The Gods in a starry
lather, goaded into escapades. I am astrological, precocious
with omens. I name the girls their terrible husbands: eight
madding bastards who go to the drink and drive their fast
cars into quarries.

And the school, our Reverent Mother: five years' time
and the novices with their currying, sheepish looks will
all be gone, their frailties and their waltzes swept massively away.

ii

The Little Sisters in their clerical caterwaul, hang
lullabies like lanterns in the rafters of the roof.

The girls here get a skin on like boiled milk.
They sponge or drudge, or sob into their stirabout,
chewing the ends of their hair.

I once tried to explain the heat death of the universe
by muddling jam into Emmeline's porridge. She hit me
with a wooden spoon.

Tonight it is raining. They were aiming paper darts
at the Pavee girl, her *pasty face* is a chalky streak,
like bird shit on a black-out curtain.

Maybe tomorrow they'll find her narrow body in the narrow
bath, stood out against the dark water like the white blaze
on the nose of a black stallion.

Or maybe she'll ascend to the stars, open
the window, climb onto the ledge. Behind her
the girls cold-creaming each other's faces, singing
along to a smuggled B-side, egging her on to *fly*
away home.

Those girls, embroidering biology with tissue and excuses,
mouthing moist idiocies at one another: *a pash, a crush, she*
spat, she cursed me. Giddy, winsome girls. And stupid.
She always liked the drastic math of distances, distances
measured by the number of holes you can fall into at
any one time.

I once tried to explain the heat death of the universe
by spooning jam into Emmeline's porridge. She hit
me. And she hit me. And she hit me.

Polhymnia

And I will bend to my service, dancing bear
in her hair shirt, slowly swayed. I am built
for scourges, fasts, and sacerdotal tasking;
for squirming thirst and high compline. I
offer up this song, my song, the big-haired
power ballad of my penance. Do not hide
your face away, oh Lord, but play the long
odds of my rescue; adjust your cloth cap,
pull on your nubby gloves, and work
the short – oh, shortest – con of my salvation.

I will stoop to my service, Lord, pretend to
a prudent recluse; to six degrees of picturesque
scrimping. Ashy-faced, crone, and erring, I
will submit. And I shall commit my lipstickless
singing; kneel with parabolised saddos, hooded
like hawks. Lord, do not turn away from me.
My narrow bed is a plank for walking, nightly.
And Sister Joan, that flat, canonical chatelaine,
crouches behind my keyhole, full of condensed
milk and malapropped spite.

Yes, I will sing in my service. When I sing
Paradise pulls from the true like a Polaroid
picture in candled resolve. This is the real
work of serving, not sweeping up our sighs
in a sooty house. Praise is rough contraband,
colours the lung. I am yarning an *ave*, red
thread and gold.

Terpsichore

No, not those girls, in a pink-white crisis of coquetry,
whose movement is all anatomical trance. Not those girls,
in crêpe and tulle, and transports; trippy telepresent swan
maidens, dizzied at a ritual, whose wings are a pillow fight
frieze of feathers, who dither and spin. No, not them. I will
have quarrelsome harbingers, stripped to their strict funery,
caustic and wan, whose dance is a railing intercourse. I will
have symmetry, a plague of symmetries. Our faces are
beacon and I will shine, louche and bruised, enshrined
in a tiered dress, in a webbed mass of antisocial blackness,
bronze. Our faces are *vévé*, brute and greased. Our bodies
will verge and rivet and churn. This is to be a haggling
dance, a dance of harm and prayer. I will not dance with
the frittering girls, pointing their snug toes, truffled in
gentrified petticoats, their small paws pandered in lavender
laps. Mine are the serpent cohort, twisting into heated
coils, superbly Tesla. My chorus is *street meat, puta madre,
valley trash*. We gloss a dance without music, the mouth
an alchemical smear. The heavy night has a headache.
We are a human heatwave, heat-weaved. Writhe to
the cadence of a knife fight, dear.

Calliope, 1985

Here it is then, girls. I'm wise enough to know when to quit, are you? Sweet girls, bonny and frantic, damning yourself with incredulous hexing. The coppers will come, as bent as spoons. Regardless, the coppers will come. Pig bastards, fascist fucks, as pushy as stage mothers. This operational egging on is endless. This one, a diva, preening his fists in a daze like a song. He's out for you, sweet girls. Pack up your homes, pack yourselves into yourselves, your sleeping bags, your Blythe Power T-shirts, agonies and cabbages. Your van is a bin of cinders now, they've lit fires under us. This field is a charmed steppe, glows, is sodden and welling. Our cars, our vans, our homes are nodes of light.

Oh sweet girls, go, through a gap in the fence, through the shoved rummage of bodies, the boys in the blame of their bodies, slumming in mud. Pass Danny, a mummy-wrapped Murphy in his sea-dog dreads, his mouth a crush, a smear, a frail and blistery scrape. Boys, girl, the dogs in their consort swarm, snapping their teeth, perforate urgently. The dogs profess a music, proliferate howls, vexed and homesick. Those pig bastards, Nazi fucks, breaking heads.

This one is virtuoso, trebles the black keys of our teeth like a Mozart. Girls, the radiant pain of a burning. A scheme of trees, black against yellow, and red, and run. I will stand my ground, stirring these fault-lines into my face, stirring tamarind and turmeric into my pot.

I mother regret, lug love like a missal, am passive, impassive, and just. Here it is then, walloped, tackled and cracked, auditioning sleep. Leave me inlaid like a Gibson guitar, acoustic and mournful and mother of pearl.

Our Lady of the Lock

From here the whole place seems so small, exhibits a shrunken
radiance, a star deformed by gravity. It's six a.m. I miss you
more than ever, and it gets harder, coming back, to Hawley,
sprawling, prematurely haunted; gaunt and Born Again, stirring
her pigeon dynasties. All along the Lock they're *cleaning house,*
moneymen smiling with a charmless tact. I know them well
and watch myself. I stand with my back to the wall. Investors
have been setting fires; their glass panels poised to fall
like guillotines. The ugly oligarchitectures coruscate with razored
light. In a white heat Camden writhes, and *punters* queue to
see the cooked skin sliding off her bones. I am left alone,
to cold defeatist festering in parks. Terraced house draw their
lairy slogans tighter round their bony shoulders. Streets are
almost empty, except I see a skinny girl, limping in gold
slingbacks, dragging a wheelie case against the traffic. She
is platinum, shattered, with Patient Zero cheekbones: Zombie.
Once she belonged somewhere, once she was beautiful. Her
wet-look shirt is torn in back, a bin bag ripped by a fox
in the night. She says she's been *evicted.* There are
government departments for precision-engineering pain. We
know this well. I'd like to tell her she is *still* beautiful. It gets
harder, coming back, sitting down beside the depthless black
emetic water. I think how we would gather here. We carried
constellations on our backs, a million flashing sliver spurs,
when we believed in *some*thing. I walk the skaggy lanes
in a summer haze like builders' tea, and all the redbrick
basements, chafing with decay, exhaling hash and malice.
I pass the khat fanatics chewing cud; teenybops, fraggle on
acid. I miss you more than ever. So little now remains:
a backed up drain, a barking dog. Developers are moving
in to sweep our sacred mess away, disown our ghosts, as if
they could. Our Lady will protect them. Our Lady of the Lock.

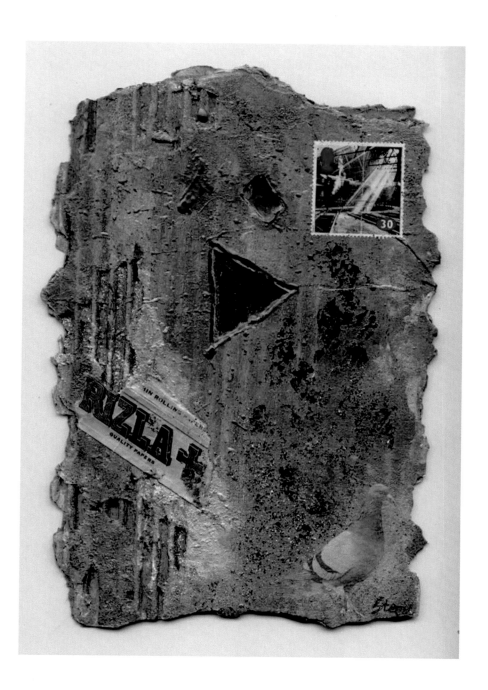

You see, I *still* believe in something. She is with us, even
now. Her skin is pallid tallow, her laugh the canal's
undertow. Wise men follow her gold teeth to Stables.
Dashboard Madonna with the peeling paint, she bends
low to the old dossers, whispers slurring Grace into
their pungent sleep. She charms the Somali loner-
boy when moth flight falters holes in the fabric of his
reason and his fist becomes a basket of knives. She
soothes the wives of drinking men with echoes
of caresses, and songs that sound like *home.* For those
who live in fear of darkened stairwells, she is the shape
of a big black dog to walk beside. And you, climbing
the wall at the top of the Market, sat on the roof in
the morning, holding court, and courting arrest,
and cupping your hands around a cone of fire. You'll follow
her too, and her tatterdemalion retinue, over the bridge
and on toward Chalk Farm, where the grass is greener,
the pastures lush. They can come, the moneymen, gutless
and devising blight; eye-fucking her facelift with violent
hunger. They think that they can claim what's ours, but
they believe in nothing and belong to nothing. They would
not know her if they saw her, if she stripped naked and
wriggled around in their laps. They see only the sodden,
stooped, accumulating ruin. They talk the fork-tongued
folklore of regeneration, gentrification. They don't know
that we survive, that I will meet you here forever, and in
sleep's velvety sufferance, on the steps of the squat
they forgot to tear down, in the knave of her church.
There's no belonging without longing. Patron Saint
of trespasses, Patroness of impossible dreams. The sky
is still unconquered; the promiscuous plenty of a brand
new day.

RAG
TOWN
GIRLS

Rag Town

Chorus: *Us learned the truth at seventeen, that love was made for beauty queens, and silly cows who all believe the shit they read in magazines...*

The man on the corner screaming: *Who'd you think you are?* And La-la was scared of him, so I kicked him square in his Sassenachers, and fuck you very much for my pains. No one is here for the fun of it. La-la and I going down the offie in pessimistic leggings with the knees bagged out because who cares anyway and why make the effort? This is the only forever we'll ever get our hands on. No love. There's no one here on whom to lavish absolutes. Love, the defeatist fan-fic of amateur porno; the dropped jaw you drag on gravel. La-la says *we was never not hungry*. Sometimes we just stay in and listen to music; we like the shy boys, furtively genderless, pouting their lisping aggro at no one. La-la lines my eye for me. My slow blink is target practice. La-la's lips are flytrap pink, then red, and green. We're rendering, extraordinary with war paint. In La-la's room, sub-tropically-postered, glossy leaves that wilt in scented heat. We've closed the windows. *Halleluiah* happens. Slow dance in odd socks. We move, distorted buoyancy. La-la's is a calm she wears like a scar. In the flat above they're screaming, a rage that sounds like running water. Constant torrent, force of nature. We smoke, we're getting slow. La-la picks her words like eyelashes. I pursue my words with tweezers. Never connect. We're staying in, not for us the strident delinquency of pulsing beats and pity fucks. Ned, his catastrophic handspan through a window in a pub. C and K and all the rest, buzzing like a game of Operation. The guilty hurt you grasp like a rose between your teeth, else slips between your ribs in an opportune alley with a boy's hand on your thigh. La-la is beautiful. By which I mean La-la is La-la, and when we lie side by side we look like we belong together – two halves of a worm that got sliced by a spade. A prayer might go like this: *Let summer not become the migraine that divides us.* Gross old men peering from behind expectant hedges. Dads that hassle us in shorts. But La-la most because I am gargoyle. A prayer might be something to do with escape. But that's not realistic. We can only run so far. The elasticity of anger, madness pushed to a tinfoil extremity, howling at the moon outside the city limits. But just outside. There is no road to trip. There is no bird's eye view. La-la is asleep. Sister from another mirror, how I've wanted in every sense repulsed enthralled the pinkish meat of you. La-la, when my jaundiced labours end and I return, empty-handed, artlessly sullen, will you always be waiting? No. There is no always. Rag Town's raving its face off again. The neckline plunges darkly. The pencil pushes back at the hand that holds it.

Rag Town Girls do Poetry

The boys was predictably lingering. You, flea-market demeanour, not benign, not even really joking. Your dress is guesswork: *sheer* is the word. I have the scarecrow's hurt mufti, a grudging velvet, wet black soil, and I have the eye's glassy art, will *screw 'em out*, the other girls, with beauties we will never have recourse to. The boys was banging on, tactless and awed, all smirking grievance, saluting the stiff red pout of you. You said: *I dunnae aim t' please.* They looked at you and trembled. Boys, girls, flaunting a mere shruggable illness. We was the two-headed Goddess of Anything Chronic. We was *a couple a' canny twats.* You trampled roses under foot. I bit the heads off bats. The hardman had a blue tattoo, a pulpy laugh. You planted your slippery, ill-advised mouth right on his thick, hot jugular. These were dark times, a bad idea was *really brilliant.* Your breath an ashy blessing as you said: *fuck me incurable in a nylon light*, with a sigh like artificial sweetener. My eyes was mood rings, mood swings, changeable and squeamish, pulsing waves of earnest malice, the shit I was eager and toxic with: Indigo! Indigo! Indigo! You took my hand in the ladies, you used a nail to trace my vein. I got a crawly lust inside of me. I got the urge to open up, to decorate with blood's black bunting, all across the mirror. You wrote: *Gimme a fix!* On the glass with a lipstick, in a richer colour than the one I run with. Omegaless, my vegan saline, super-unleaded, a diet shake. You was laughing, and I locked on you: gaunt, ecstatic, bandying about like a dying swan. You, haughtiness, promiscuous swank; a grin like a lizard: from rust to gold, cold-blooded rhetoric, sea-change, disco. You was an unpronounceable name, more night than shade, and I was lusciously poisoned. The boys was boo-hooing into their cups. You was the near-death dazzle of cheekbones. I was in the spotlight like an ant under a magnifying glass, tiny black body about to fry. You was as cool as a crock sink, you was wearing running water in the shape of male tears. You was paragon and ghastly like a figure on a tomb. I was a gargoyle, yellow and crumbling, croaking with a gap-toothed, boggle-eyed discord. We was cackling like witches; I was hooked and stooped and skinny; you was all shook up with mega-mega sorcery. When we was up at the front a straggly clarity came inching across my brain like a sprig of barbed wire. All eyes was sucked towards you, all their metal fillings was drawn in a glittering line towards your powerful magnets. You was lit up like a super villain. I was your hunch-backed assistant. You made the lightning crack, and I mopped up the electrical spills. When we was done you gathered my arms like firewood, and the boys goggled, and the girls goggled. You super-collided my forehead in a kiss. La-la, who loves ya, baby?

Rag Town Girls are Star Fuckers

Because God, back then they was *so cool*. Everyone was *so cool*. And the frontman rolled up his sleeves in the spotlight, curling his lip back, flexing his risk. And we was *so cool*. And we wasn't screaming, we was sucking our cool enthusiasm up through straws. Mine's the murkiest rum in recorded history. La-la's on vodka, a tight, hot buzz you wriggle into. Because God, back then they was *so cool*. And he's talking to us. And we're talking to him. And my voice falls out of me, decanted in splashes. And when the men in torn black jeans carry the wide black boxes solemnly about it is like a funeral in a silent film. He presides at a private grief, head turned away: half vampire, and half priest. La-la kisses his ring finger. The players of instruments assemble themselves like Argonauts, awaiting their turn. Because God, back then they was *so cool*. And our eyes was wide on a gluttony of dust. We lacked and murmured, wanted things. We was *so cool*. Undress, and the long spine jukes like a hare, yellow in a narrow sunrise in a hotel bedroom. *Cool*, worshipful and wooing. Bitten, kissed on, mawkishly convulsed; paused, posed in a roseate Polaroid. La-la is a white head on a black background like a pirate flag. And his songs like rancorous parables. And his hands in my hair. And his lip ring, septic metal; blissy swagger, we are punctured and crooned to. Oh, *so cool*. Girls with the plush breasts of pheasants, Flemish and still-life, artfully deceased. We pass between hands; we have the smooth green curvature of bottles. He pushes his thumb through me like an egg. The other boys make assaults on the satin.

Rag Town Girls go Dancing

For the longest time, the face you palm like a precious stone, repeating the words *rose quartz* to yourself in an undertone. There was a love we ripened like amnesia, a big forgetting that filled in all the blanks. But then it was the afterward, the after wood: afflicted, skint, surplus and deserted in a world with too many women in already. On those days what else to do but squat before your bijou vanity table and make unflinching inventory, from mishap to disaster. On those days you apply green goo in a semi-circular motion, leave for fifteen minutes, then peel your face away from your face like the skin from hot, boiled milk. On those days you get ready. On those days you go out. *Out* isn't what it used to be: here comes C and C's disaffected pronouns, lungs crushed up like empties inside C's binder. C swaggers with the bullish musk C's drunk on. C swaggers. K swaggers. Everybody swaggers. *Out* is our brash disorder. *Out* is the gory logic we've feathered our brains with, everybody waiting for a violent shock. K holds out her hand for one split atom, two, three, an anti-social sufficiency of pills. Lukewarm worming dusk, and the club is getting moody, zoological. That happens. In the dark the faces of your girlfriends glow like orange pips: white, Americanly ominous, terminally undelighted. *Out* is grabbing La-la's hand and running through the green emergency exit to score a more decaffeinated atmosphere; it's laying your head in her lap in desolate homage, sucking the red wine stains from her sateen skirt. *Out* is the few loony stars on your walk back home, fading all patchy like a temporary tattoo. *Out* is the brittle, twitching fanfare blared from phones across the fountain, not quite *Careless Whisper,* as you kick off your shoes and declare undying lust. *Out* is you, belligerently messianic in the mid-nineties, La-la howling *come down* as you climb the Spire to death or glory. *Out* is more or less fucked; it's a fight with baldies, sleepy-eyed as stoics on the nightbus, in the lanes. It's you, Titan with head-wound 'cause you was spewing the sulphurous morning up, 'cause you wanted the world, 'cause you couldn't keep your big mouth shut.

Rag Town Girls do Unemployment

Somnambulous afternoon, slump-buttocked and grouchy. *C'mon Ned*, and you and La-la drag him off the couch. The high-street is sniffable, gluey, leaves your appetite in shreds, but anyway. And you're passing the burger bar, and the residents are foddering like zombies inside, and through the plate-glass you can see a woman, mid-forties, has cancer, her head all swollen, white and gummy like a sucked dumpling. And Ned remembers his Ma and wipes his nose on his sleeve. It's afternoon alright, with emergency services making a rock opera out of helicopters; a front bumper on a traffic island, gleaming like a horse's jawbone, picked cold. Incident tape extends anemone tendrils with a deep-sea delicacy, yellow, black and blue. Cars up on bricks are basking like sharks. The pawn shop with its windows smashed, a mayday of semi-precious metals, Community Support looking on like daffodils in high-vis. This is the world. You follow the one way system out of town. You're *going where the weather suits your clothes*, this from La-la, laughing. In the park you loll on the smogged up grass, or slouch on incoherent benches, grimed with arbitrary passions, and with birdshit. You share a tepid tea, watch junkies disappearing down into the public toilets like white rabbits, consulting invisible watches, muttering under their smeggy breath how *late* they are. It's as afternoon as it's going to get, the park becomes capered with dogs off leads, an English bull with his log-flume face makes a fuss of you. He is white all over, with a Gorbachev birthmark in brilliant raspberry. You decide to adore him. The women come next, stylishly adrift but miserable with it, their hair ornate in failure, scrape-backed and flammable, they dangle kids like shoulder bags, customised toddlers with teeth as straight as the edge of a credit card. They whoop but do not smile, a mannered joy they act out like an injury. You decide to go home, take a shower, rinse the dreggy sweat you are disgusted by. In the shower the removal of hair is like the unblocking of a sink. Over your shoulder, La-la, intent on the mirror, undoing her make-up in chess moves; unwrapping her reflection like a crappy Christmas present.

Rag Town Girls see God

There he is, eyes half closed, doing the math of a difficult miracle, wrist-wearied, leaning into his swig, his pull of smoke. We assume he is God. He reminds us of a man we once knew: slender and insulted by life, mixing his blessings like strong drink, suicidally agile, tying a nimble noose the minute your back was turned. Not all kinds of pain are soluble in water, this is a thing God would know. There he is, polishing a bad mood like a monocle, in dive bars, erring on the side of squalor, as is usual, succumbing to a bleak urge now and then, a typical thrill, blood's red adventure, cuts himself or dallies a sulky vein. He's writing on a napkin. He's writing in the back of an exercise book on green graph paper. This gives his words a barometric feel. Poems, possibly. A long phrase escalates like science: pressure, rise and fall. There he is. We assume he's God. Who else could he be? His blue eyes like stains under black light, a half smile through a vaporous reverie. He reminds us of a man who was always leaving his door ajar like *youthful promise unfulfilled.* He reminds us of a man, decisively hysterical in hospitals on Friday nights. We came to see him. La-la held his hand in an ambulance once, and other girls, entangled attentions he grew tired of and soon. We remember him, passed out at a party, Lugosian in repose, those folded hands, those overweening teeth. C had saddled him. Others too, young and drunk, with slack or sculpted mouths, trashy and vamping, pretending to be grown. God, yes. He absorbed their adoration like the sea absorbing snow. There he is, tremulous willpower, Crombie coat. When he wrote it down, when he pulled you to him in a bouncer's embrace. Love as a grunting headlock you cannot wriggle out of. Better to lie still, snug and grim against the reeling two-step of his heart. If he had a heart. La-la says *yes.* I am inclined to contrary opinion. Watch him now, groping at dominoes, putting forth paranoia like pine needles. He is the same, but elongated. There is prayer, and then there is a deadlier efficacy. God, in his Kingdom. God, in his Wisdom. God, in his window seat. He let himself go.

Rag Town Girls Don't Want to be in your Shitty Fucking Magazine/Anthology/Stable of Wanky, Middle-class Poets Anyhow

Writing a poem is not like painting a nail. But you like things with *proper edges,* words obscenely organised. We take our rejection letters to bed, spend weekends floundering a vowel, and *how to get this better?* Ours, the unstruttable slang of profitless margins. We belong on the *out* of things, prowling and gaspy. And picking a side is like picking a scab – the inner arm, its crumbs of blood –. Writing a poem no one wants. Insomnia's aberrant artifice, night after night. It is taking out an ad in the paper: *I have built my house of straw!* Our poems are prefab and flammable, no one's moving in. You like things with *proper edges.* The world is not something to traverse, but something to survive. To keep us on our toes the city varies its monsters, but sex keeps harping its long, fatal theme. *Residents,* but not *citizens. Relatives,* but not *family.* Blame is the only thing that belongs between us equally. La-la says the poem comes away from her like an enchanted shadow detaching. I disagree. I think it is more like tearing a plaster off a deep cut to the thumb. You like things with *proper edges.* You would never mistake *violation* for *volition.* In the bathroom mirror we try out our Poetry Voices. Poetry Voices are needed for the receiving of prizes. I've been perfecting a cough that sounds like crutches being kicked. La-la's laugh has stripped a turkey carcass down to the fats in under sixteen minutes. Now we need the outfits. We will wear white, immaculate as rabbits. La-la's is the Roman toga of the downward thumb. Mine is a sheet with holes cut in for eyes. Writing a poem is not like planting a kiss. Or a tree. How to get this better? Intelligence a sauce we suck from fingers, with fuck me haircuts in a youth club. How to slide right out of yourself, like a limousine pulling away from the curb? How to deny the flight of stairs you took to the roof on windy days, when you wanted to float, kite caught in a whiplash of its own making? How to fake it? How to keep it in, that jittery, impassable grief? *Don't scratch yourselves, girls. Bathe. Point your toes.* Glowing in a backward light cast by everything you flee from. You like *proper edges,* incline a tin ear to the shrug and flutter of our debateable music. If we could only sing like you, a proficient, accredited language. But we can't, so we won't. La-la lit a fire instead. It ate a hole in everything.

Notes on Rag Town Girls

By Fran Lock

We have the right, and we deserve the space in which to be angry. I started writing the Rag Town sequence with this one thought looping endlessly in my head.

The poems came about in the wake of International Women's Day, and my disillusionment with what I perceived, and still perceive, as an ongoing cultural project to make feminism palatable and popular, and in doing so leave behind those women and girls who are most in need of its radical and revolutionary message.

Did you know that International Women's Day used to be called International Working Women's Day? True story. But somewhere along the way it became unacceptable to openly acknowledge how class dynamics contribute to sex-based oppression. I've bought this up often in the last four or five years and with each iteration it has been seen as more and more divisive. It's divisive, for example, to say that white, settled, middle-class women "escape" from unlovable and undervalued domestic labour at the expense of working-class women, immigrant women, women in poverty. It's divisive to advocate for, to demand, a version of feminism that isn't about "individual choice", but collective liberation, for all women, not just pretty, white rich ones.

This fills me with despair. And the media coverage of IWD fills me with increasing despair each year, as I wonder aloud at the lack of working-class female voices allowed to proliferate and express themselves; at the lack of exposure given to women led grass-roots community activism, or the problems effecting a significant number of women and girls living and working in poverty.

There was no celebration either, of female working-class art or voice, or their unpredictable and vibrant networks. There was nothing around that captured the music and the beauty of women's lives as they were really lived, the things we find to enrich us and sustain us. This infuriated me.

Rag Town became a place in which the joys, frustrations, miseries and victories of "unacceptable", imperfect and angry women and girls can be told. The poems speak of grind, grot and exploitation, but from the inside, with resilience and élan. There's a refusal to give in, a determination to swagger and saunter and spin through their difficult lives and less than lovely town. This resilience is something I've aspired to in my own life, something I witness every day in my family and friends. The poems are meant to stand as testament to those people, to reflect the ambiguities, the hardships and pleasures of growing up poor and growing up "other" and growing up a girl. I wanted to write something that would make a space for and honour anger, but also kinship, cohort, solidarity and music.

Steev's pictures capture this determination to dance and sing; they show the creativity and flare of individuals rising above their circumstances to find and experience moments of joy. This matters to me. Joy is revolutionary work, because there are those who would deny it to people in poverty, those who think that unemployed or minimum wage existence has some moral obligation to be a tedious, soulless, pleasureless grind. We have to be the first to acknowledge that we deserve better.

The girls in Rag Town are often unhappy, are as vulnerable and exploited as many working-class girls, but they sing the complexities of that exploitation, and insist upon their right to be seen in other ways, as complex, nuanced and profound as their middle-class counterparts.

Notes on the Muses

By Fran Lock

Melpomene (the Muse of Tragedy): Her "tragedy" is both the past she carries, and her violent separation from it. She is someone who cannot reconcile herself to the world or to her life as it is. The speaker is someone who cannot return "home" but who cannot make peace with the inadequacies and horrors of her present exile either. I was thinking of how Edward Said described exile as "the unhealable rift forced between a human being and a native place, between the self and its true home: its essential sadness can never be surmounted."

Euterpe, known as the "giver of delight" (Muse of Music, and later Lyric Poetry): One of only two specifically historical pieces. This poem came to me in response to a story I was told about the unsolved murder of two Traveller women, somewhere near Kilsheelan during the 1950s. I couldn't verify the story, and suspect it's something of an apocryphal tale, but its existence struck me as a kind of informal acknowledgement of the tensions and toxicities that bubble and boil beneath the surface of communal life. This is a poem about hypocrisy, bigotry and blame, but more importantly to me, it's a poem about how something that has great beauty, sweetness and meaning to the initiated can be degraded and debased by deliberate misinterpretation. It's a poem about drawing strength and pleasure from a frisson of risk, about the courage not to be cowed, about daring to dance. It's a poem about everything irrevocably lost in translation.

Thalia (Muse of Comedy): This is my favourite of the nine pieces. Her monologue is funny, but she knows it's funny, and we're laughing with and not at her. She has this hectic, slightly mad vivacity, which is an expression of her as yet undefeated desire to see and know and experience everything. I love her for her headstrongness, her determination to spread joy and hijinx. For me she also represents sorority, laughter being that which binds her sisterhood together. She uses a lot of theatrical slang because her personal style is pure Vaudeville. She is a composite of many of the teenage girls in my life. In their inventiveness, flare and frivolity I find hope.

Clio (Muse of History): This is perhaps the most complex of the sequence. I was thinking a lot about the tensions and collisions between cultural heritage and personal past. In Ireland, in particular, History is often glorious, while the private lives and living memories of people and of families are littered with miseries, disillusionments and griefs. Clio is constantly measuring herself and her own foreshortened perception of History against the grand ancestral memory her mother was the keeper of. She blames herself, uses the word "poshrat", meaning "half-breed", imagining that if she belonged more completely to her culture and its traditions she would be able to access a better story, a better memory. The piece reflects my own ambiguous attitude to and fraught relationship with the myth of Ireland and Irishness. Also, implicit in the poem are questions about what constitutes a "history", and what is worthy of remembering.

Erato (Muse of Erotic Poetry, Love Poetry, and of Mime): I imagined Erato as one of a long line of Miss Connemara contestants; a beauty queen never allowed to be anything but beautiful, expected to turn being looked at into an art form and not particularly pleased about it. She's the parallel of Thalia, but Erato is imprisoned by her identity rather than inspired by it. The beauty contest is to me one the most anachronistic and baffling aspects of Irish culture. It baffles the poem's speaker too, who feels herself enslaved to and engulfed by decades of stifling tradition. Erato is female sexuality exploited in the service of cultural myth. "Not *lovely*", she says, "but *typical*", although beneath the surface she is anything but. The idea of Mime in this context signifies to me a going through the motions, the making of a series of contentless and hollow gestures towards tradition. Erato knows she's not the image in the flashbulb, but equally she does not know what she might be without it.

Urania/Ourania (sometimes the Muse of Astronomy, sometimes the Muse of Astrology, sometimes both): I cheated here, imagining the duel aspects of Urania/Ourania as identical twins, two girls enrolled in convent school, one of whom is very much concerned with the illicit practice of casting the tarot, and her sister who is held in fascinated thrall by science. They embody the tensions between the "rational" and the magical or mythic world, but also between culture and occulture, personifying several kinds of "forbidden" knowledge (the tarot itself and the reading of signs and portents, the secret world of schoolgirls with its ciphers and private signs, and physics, the enormity of which is another kind of challenge to the dominance of religion). For me these two represent the ways in which knowledge survives and takes roots, makes its incursions into a culture that is trying to stifle it or stamp it out. Urania sees "civilisation" itself as an unessential relic that will be "swept away". Her knowledge is older, but will endure.

Polhymnia (Muse of Hymns or Sacred Songs): This piece occupies a similarly uneasy intersection between Catholic faith and Pagan tradition. She too has a secret inner life, but hers does not exist in subversive undercurrent, rather it is repressed, except at vital moments when she is allowed to sing; in singing the two halves of her heritage are allowed to synchronise, to co-exist. In singing she becomes whole. For Polhymnia as for myself, all songs and acts of singing are inherently sacred and healing.

Terpsichore (Muse of Dance): My Terpsichore embodies everything that is menacing or destabilising about "otherness". In her dancing there is a violence and sexual threat, a grim revelling in the role of dangerous outsider, of being beyond society, its expectations and constraints. That is not to say she is a "powerful" figure in the usual sense, but that, being denied legitimate power she nevertheless finds ways of exerting influence, of using peoples' assumptions against them. She is underestimated, so she cultivates that underestimation and turns it to her advantage. I am not interested in excusing the sexual exploitation of women with some catch-all notion of "agency", but I do want to write about the ways in which women and girls maintain their dignity, and the strategies they adopt that allow them to survive. Terpsichore's dancing is a strategy, it walks the knife-edge between violence and sexual desire, and in doing so gives vent to her rage.

Calliope (Muse of Epic Poetry and of Eloquence): Of course Calliope has the last word. Hers is the only other poem with a fixed date. The action of the piece takes place at an eviction in 1985, recalling the now infamous Battle of the Beanfield, but the "battle" could be any, and it echoes all such scenes, now too numerous to mention. There is something tongue-in-cheek about this piece. A Muse of Eloquence being given to multi-clausal swear streams is intended as humour, but also there's something about the brutality of the eviction that makes her overstep her role, that causes her carefully constructed persona to topple and break. There are some situations in the face of which language is inadequate. State violence is one of them.

Calliope's battle closes the collection but it also begins it again, in Tragedy, with Melpomene, and the things that she's seen that will not give her peace. In a way I wish I was ending on a happier note. I would have liked to give Thalia the last page, or Urania, or maybe even Terpsichore, but sudden and shocking displacement underscores every aspect of these women's lives. Not just Traveller women. Not just migrant women and refugees. All working-class women. Whose locatedness is never stable, always fraught. Calliope's piece is a reminder and a call to arms. Keep moving girls, keep searching, for a better belonging, a better road, a better home.

Notes on the Collages

By Steev Burgess

I've known Fran for about seven years now, after first seeing her read at Y Tuesday, a poetry club I used to run with friends. Fran and I would often go on 'derives' around different parts of London, either on the way to a poetry gig or sometimes to a place I knew she would find interesting. I was always intrigued to see how the things seen and talked about as we wended our way would crop up again in her poetry, sometimes within days, sometimes much later, in fragmented form, as if in a dream.

The idea for 'muses' probably started on the South Bank, behind the Oxo building where the muses are listed on an old brick wall and where I took a photo of Fran as Melpomene – the muse of tragedy. Perhaps the large, weathered, warehouse wall, with peeling paintwork influenced my pictures in this book subconsciously too, as they are very different to the collaged Arcadian visions that I've been working on over the last decade. I always found my darkest and most melancholy feelings went into poetry and song, and my art provided windows of escape and inspiration.

When Fran asked me if I'd like to work on this book I was really happy but slightly worried: you surely can't illustrate poetry that is so full of visual imagery anyway? I found that the solution was to represent the atmosphere, and bring the muses to the streets of modern day London (Camden town in particular) where I live and Fran once lived in a crumbling Georgian squat. I wanted to evoke the damaged walls of a squat, with naked wires and broken plasterwork painted in my pictures, painted over as people were wont to do as well. Many squatters I've known have been extremely creative folk and never wasted time before decorating the rooms in the most individual fashion.

I decided to unite the two halves of the book with one style of imagery. Though a Londoner, I knew the decaying old northern 'rag towns' as I was once a football photographer. The muses get replaced by the rag town girls in their desperate quest for the heart of Saturday night, with night club and acid house colours slowly creeping in as the book progresses.